S

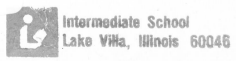

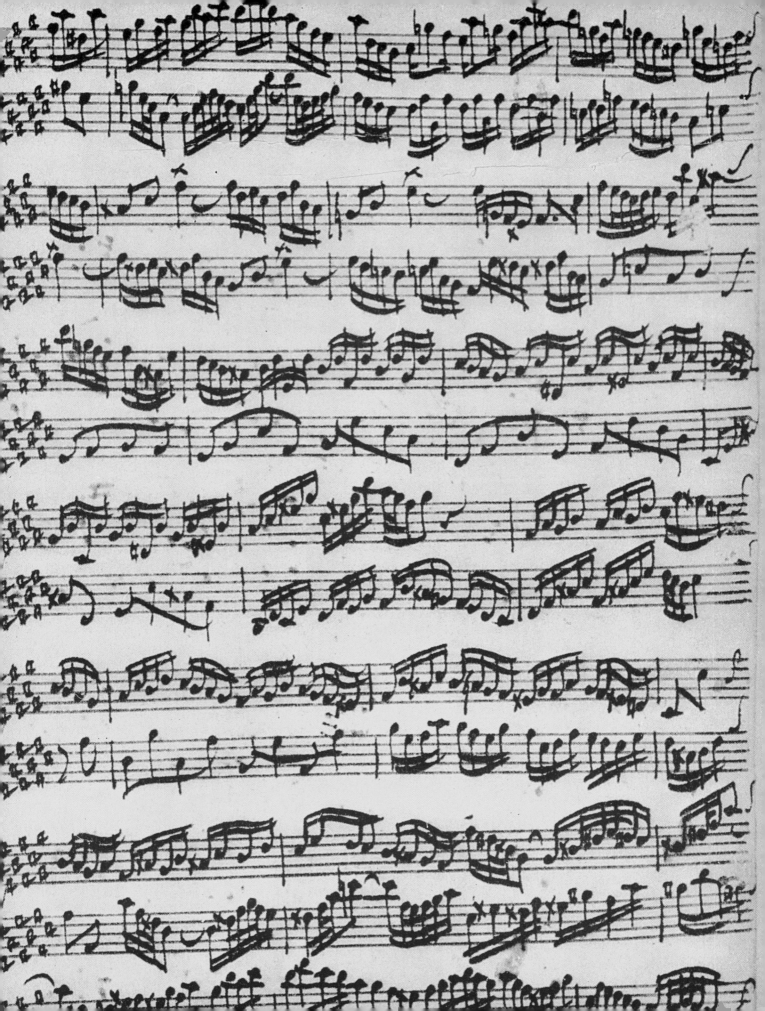

Previous page: A page from the score of the Well-Tempered Clavier. Bach composed these 24 Preludes and Fugues in 1722. He was testing a new system of tuning keyboard instruments by composing in "all tone and semi-tones".

Below: A view of the marketplace in Leipzig as it was in the 17th century.

BACH
and His World

Cynthia Millar

SILVER BURDETT

Contents

Editorial

Author

Cynthia Millar

Editors

Jane Olliver

Caroline Royds

Illustrators

Owain Bell

Roger Phillips

For Stanley

Left: This engraving (1730) shows a maker of stringed instruments. Among the instruments he carries are a lute, violin and cello.

A KINGFISHER BOOK

Published in the United States by Silver Burdett Company, Morristown, New Jersey.

1980 Printing

ISBN 0-382-06378-3

Designed and produced by Grisewood & Dempsey Limited, Grosvenor House, 141-143 Drury Lane, London WC2.

The Baroque Era

The word Baroque, meaning highly decorated, was first used to describe the architecture of the period 1620–1750, but applies equally well to the other arts and to the period as a whole.

Europe, shaken up by the new ideas and discoveries of the Renaissance, was seeking to assimilate them, while being constantly interrupted by political upheaval. It was an age of contrasts. In peacetime, notably at the Court of Charles I in England, and of Louis XIV, France's Sun King, entertainment was never more spectacular nor lavish, as the courtiers tried to forget the horrors of war. The musical language expanded, opera was born, and it was a sign of a ruler's riches and position to employ musicians to compose and perform to order. The Church was the oldest patron of all, and it was in its service, in German towns, that Bach composed and performed almost exclusively. Far removed from the competition and extravagance of the French and Italian courts, Bach, the greatest composer of his age, evolved a style of his own, combining the best of current Italian and French ideas with the German church tradition.

Much of the theatrical music of the period was written for special occasions and has now been lost; but the music of the modest Bach, unknown outside Germany during his lifetime, is now accepted as one of the finest, most glorious expressions of the Baroque spirit.

The center of the Grand Avenue at Sans-souci Palace near Potsdam. This round colonnade is in the Baroque style, decorated with patterns and sculpture.

Bach's World

Bach never traveled outside Germany and took no part in shaping the rapidly changing world around him. When he was born, Germany was still reeling from the damage done by the Thirty Years War (1618–1648). Yet, by the time he died, England was already feeling the effects of the Industrial Revolution which heralded the modern age; and in France the "enlightened" reasoning of the philosophers was already causing the unrest which erupted in the revolution of 1789. It was an age of contrasts – of vast riches and unimaginable poverty; of scientific advance and primitive methods. Bach's conscientiousness blinded him to all but the carrying out of the tasks he was set.

SCOTLAND

● Edinburgh

Arkwright
1732–92
(Inventor)

NORTH SEA

IRELAND

ENGLAND

Goldsmith
1728–74
(Writer)

● Dublin

Wedgwood
1730–95
(Potter)

Congreve
1670–1729
(Playwright)

Swift
1667–1745
(Writer)

Bunyan
1628–88
(Writer)

John Wesley
1703–91
(Preacher)

Gainsborough
1727–88
(Painter)

WALES

Gray
1716–71
(Poet)

Hogarth
1697–1764
(Painter)

NETHERL

Wren
1632–1723
(Architect)

Fielding
1707–54
(Writer)

Amsterdam

Plymouth ●

● London

Defoe
1660–1731
(Writer)

Purcell
1659–95
(Composer)

Pope
1688–1744
(Poet)

Antwerp ●

Reynolds
1723–92
(Painter)

● Lille

● B

● Rouen

Seine

Telem
1681–
(Com

● Paris

Louis XIV
1638–1715
Sun King

Voltaire
1694–1778
(Writer)

Haydr
1732–
(Com

Loire

Racine
1639–99
(Dramatist)

● Dijon

FRANCE

Watteau
1684–1721
(Painter)

Geneva

Lyons ●

Rousse
1712–7
(Philos
and wr

● Bordeaux

Montesquieu
1689–1755
(Writer)

Chardin
1699–1779
(Painter)

Garonne

Rhône

● Marse

Ebro

Douro

PYRENEES

● Zaragoza

PORTUGAL

Guadiana

● Madrid

● Barcelona

● Lisbon

Tagus

SPAIN

Guadalquivir

● Seville

MEDITERRANEAN SEA

NORWAY

Oslo

Stockholm

SWEDEN

RUSSIA

DENMARK • Copenhagen

Lübeck
Hamburg
Bremen

Kant
1724–1804
(Philosopher)

Elbe

Weser

Berlin

Oder

Vistula

ologne

onn **Goethe**
1749–1832
(Writer)
• Frankfurt

•Weimar

• Leipzig

• Dresden

• Prague

HOLY ROMAN EMPIRE

• Nuremberg

Gluck
1714–87
(Composer)

trasbourg

Danube

• Munich

Zurich

Handel
1685–1759
(Composer)

• Salzburg

• Vienna

ALPS

Tiepolo
1692–1770
(Painter)

Canaletto
1697–1768
(Painter)

• Milan

Po Verona

• Venice

Genoa

• Bologna

A Scarlatti
1659–1725
(Composer)

Vivaldi
1678–1741
(Composer)

D.Scarlatti
1683–1757
(Composer)

Tiber

• Rome

ITALY

• Naples

Bernini
1598–1680
(Sculptor and
architect)

• Palermo

Weser

•Celle
•Hanover

Elbe

Berlin
•Brandenburg

•Köthen

• Leipzig

• Mühlhausen

Eisenach •

• Erfurt

• Weimar
• Jena

Dresden•

Ohrdruf

• Arnstadt

THURINGIA

• Frankfurt

*Above: A map showing
Thuringia in central
Germany, where Bach and
his family lived.
Left: An engraving of the
portrait of Martin Luther
(1483–1546), by Cranach.
With his nailing of the 95
Theses to the door of
Wittenberg Cathedral,
Luther set in motion the
Reformation in Europe.
Below: Salzburg Trinity
Church, a fine example of
German Baroque
architecture.*

The Family of Bach

The world into which Johann Sebastian Bach was born was a very different one from ours. Transport was slow and uncomfortable. Coaches were expensive and, as a result, the poorer people, who had to travel on foot, did so as seldom as possible, often not straying far from their birthplaces. Because of this, certain families, once settled in a region, remained and multiplied there; and so it was with the Bachs in the German province of Thuringia.

When in 1735, Bach traced his family back, he reached his great-great-grandfather, Veit Bach. He was a miller who had left Hungary in the 16th century to escape persecution for his Lutheran ideas, and had settled in Wechmar. It is possible though, that he was in fact returning to his birthplace and that there had been Bachs in the region before him. Bach writes of him playing his cittern (a kind of lute) in time to the mill-wheel, suggesting that this was the beginning of music in his family.

Bach's choice of career was by no means an original one in his family, for Bachs were well-established court, church and town musicians. A number of them held full-time professional posts, while others combined playing for special occasions with another job. Conditions varied – a post as organist or choirmaster would often include firewood and provisions, sometimes even a place to live, as well as a salary.

However, it is essential to remember that in those days musicians did not put on airs; composition and performance were crafts to be learned – like cobbling shoes or weaving. It was necessary for them to be apprenticed to learn the trade and to form guilds to protect their rights.

Some jobs were naturally more highly regarded than others. Bach himself was conscious of a lowering of prestige as well as wages when he accepted the post of Cantor at St. Thomas's in Leipzig, after working for the princes of Weimar and Köthen. But Bach's genius lay in turning every occasion to his purpose. His life was difficult and often unhappy, his triumphs small, yet, out of these limitations, he created great music.

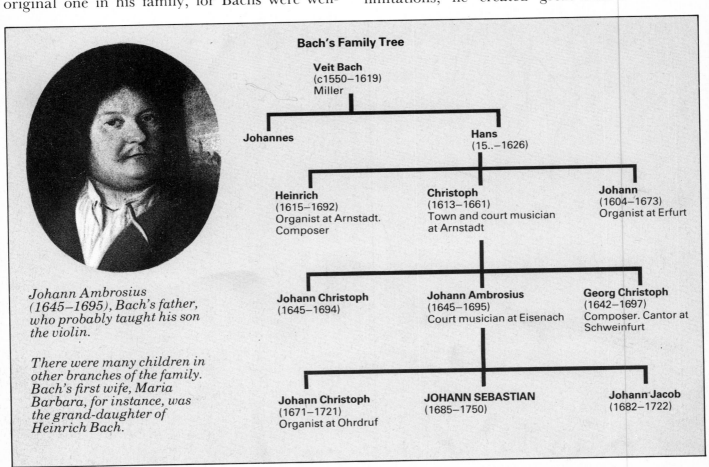

Johann Ambrosius (1645–1695), Bach's father, who probably taught his son the violin.

There were many children in other branches of the family. Bach's first wife, Maria Barbara, for instance, was the grand-daughter of Heinrich Bach.

Bach's Family Tree

Veit Bach
(c1550–1619)
Miller

Johannes

Hans
(15..–1626)

Heinrich
(1615–1692)
Organist at Arnstadt.
Composer

Christoph
(1613–1661)
Town and court musician
at Arnstadt

Johann
(1604–1673)
Organist at Erfurt

Johann Christoph
(1645–1694)

Johann Ambrosius
(1645–1695)
Court musician at Eisenach

Georg Christoph
(1642–1697)
Composer. Cantor at
Schweinfurt

Johann Christoph
(1671–1721)
Organist at Ohrdruf

JOHANN SEBASTIAN
(1685–1750)

Johann Jacob
(1682–1722)

Luther and the Reformation

Martin Luther, the greatest influence on Bach's thinking, was born 200 years before Bach in Eisleben in Germany. A devout Christian, his one great aim was to make religion understandable to ordinary people. Out of this grew the Reformation in Germany and the birth of the Protestant Church. At the beginning of the 16th century, the long church services were conducted in Latin, which the people could not understand. Luther translated the Mass into German, altering and shortening it considerably. He also introduced what he called chorales (what we would call hymns) which the congregation learned and sang. The verses were either specially composed or taken from existing poems and texts, and then set to the music of folksongs and religious tunes. It is startling to find that the great chorale tune that punctuates Bach's *St. Matthew Passion* started life as a song about a man unhappy in love.

Luther believed that music had a semi-magical quality and was second only to religion in importance. As a result, at all Protestant schools, any boy with the least aptitude, was taught to sing and play an instrument. As well as studying the Bible, the scores of old masters were painstakingly copied so that students might learn from them.

Right: This 17th-century engraving shows an organ-maker. He is surrounded by the different parts which make up the finished instrument. The pipe he is holding must be measured exactly to produce the right note.

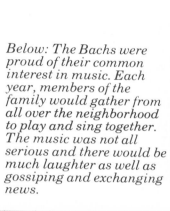

Below: The Bachs were proud of their common interest in music. Each year, members of the family would gather from all over the neighborhood to play and sing together. The music was not all serious and there would be much laughter as well as gossiping and exchanging news.

Early Years

Bach was born in Eisenach on March 21, 1685. He learned the violin from his father and enjoyed participating in the family's music-making as a young child, but his youth was clouded by unhappiness. His mother died when he was only nine and, although his father remarried in order that someone should manage the house and take care of the children, he too was dead within a year. Without financial support, Bach's stepmother had to send young Bach and his brother, Johann Jacob, to live with their eldest brother, Johann Christoph. He was the organist of St. Michael's church in Ohrdruf, 50 miles away.

Here Bach began to learn to play the keyboard, but his brother was a painstakingly slow teacher and the boy grew impatient. He knew of a manuscript of music by the most famous living composers which Johann Christoph kept locked in a lattice-fronted cabinet. Undeterred by his brother's strictness, Bach managed to extract the manuscript every night and copy it by moonlight, a bit at a time, for six months. Unfortunately, Johann Christoph found out about it after he had finished and confiscated Bach's work.

Above right: The old two-storied house in Eisenach in which Bach was born. The house is now a museum.

Below: An engraving of Eisenach showing the Wartburg, an ancient castle which towered above the town. Here Bach first went to school at the age of eight, and learned to read and write in Latin and German as well as studying theology.

Johann Christoph's family was growing all the time and it became difficult to support his brothers as well as his own children. He arranged for Johann Jacob to be apprenticed to his father's successor as Court and Town musician in Eisenach. The music master at Bach's school suggested that the boy should join the special choir at the famous music school in Lüneburg, 60 miles to the north.

At Lüneburg, Bach came under a host of new influences. Although his voice broke after a few months in the choir, he made himself useful as a violinist and as an accompanist on the organ and other keyboard instruments. Inspired by his teacher, George Böhm, Bach resolved to become a great organist. He began to compose music for the organ and to travel to hear neighboring organists play. Legend has it that on a journey home from Hamburg, Bach, footsore and unable to afford a meal, was sitting outside an inn when two herrings' heads dropped to the ground in front of him. Curious, he picked them up and discovered in each a Danish ducat from a kindhearted stranger – money enough for many meals.

Hearing that an organ had just been finished at the New Church in Arnstadt, Bach asked permission to try it out. The church officials were so impressed by his skill that they offered him the post of organist on the spot. So, in August 1703, at the age of 18, Bach was put in charge of a choir and organ of his own.

Above: The interior of St. Michael's Church in Lüneburg, as it looked to the young Bach. Outside it had a brick tower with a coppered cupola, a steep roof and tall windows. Bach must have found the building very inspiring after the simplicity of his brother's church in Ohrdruf.

Below: The city of Hamburg, 15 miles northwest of Lüneburg. Bach walked there one summer holiday to hear Jan Adams Reinken play on the great organ of St. Catherine's Church. Reinken, a man in his 80s, improvised magnificently and Bach returned home inspired.

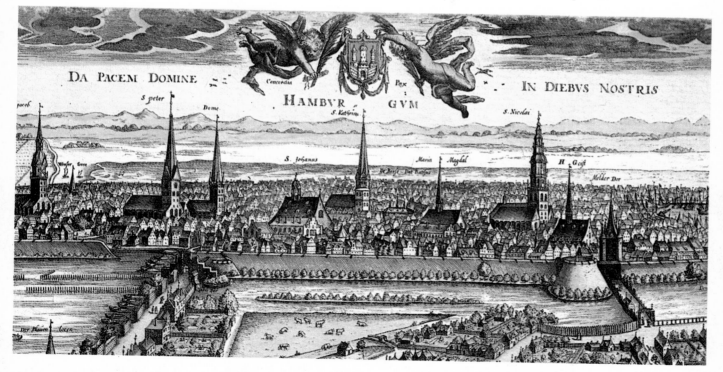

Bach the Organist

While Bach was quick to guide and inspire an intelligent pupil, he was unable to tolerate slackness, stupidity or disorder, and he soon became an unpopular choirmaster. He would have much preferred to be left alone to play the organ and compose.

After a scuffle in the street with the church bassoonist, whom Bach had insulted, the composer asked for a month's leave to journey north to hear the famous organist Dietrich Buxtehude in Lübeck. He was allowed to go in October 1705, and arrived in time to hear the famous *Abendmusik* (Evening Music) which Buxtehude conducted on five Sundays before Christmas. The spectacular effects achieved on these dramatic evenings made a deep impression on the young man, as did the contact with Buxtehude himself. Wrapped up in these new experiences, Bach lost all sense of time, and it was the end of January before he started for home. On his way he stopped to visit Reinken in Hamburg and Böhm in Lüneburg.

Trouble was brewing in Arnstadt, however. His long absence, of four months instead of four weeks, had displeased the authorities. Furthermore, his playing had changed since his meeting with Buxtehude. Instead of introducing the chorale by a customary snatch of a recognizable tune (as is done in church today), Bach extended his chorale preludes into patterns woven about the melody, mixed with trills, runs and flourishes. He indulged in flights of fancy between verses as well, so that the congregation had no idea when to begin to sing. Asked to mend his ways, Bach went to the

Above: Bach playing the simple organ at Arnstadt. The secret of great organ playing, apart from technique, of which Bach was a master, and independence of hands and feet, is to learn the art of combining different kinds of sounds in an endless number of satisfying ways. This is called the art of registration and requires adaptability, taste and discretion.

other extreme. His preludes became, instead, so short that the verses took the congregation by surprise. On finding his superiors so unsympathetic, Bach searched for, and found, another position at St. Blasius, Mühlhausen, in September 1707.

A legacy from his uncle meant that he could afford to marry his cousin, Maria Barbara, who, the church council complained, had been heard singing to his accompaniment in the organ loft. The wedding took place at nearby Dornheim in 1707.

Bach had only been at Mühlhausen for a year when he was offered the post of chapel musician to the Duke of Weimar. He saw this new job as an opportunity "to pursue the object which concerns me most, the betterment of church music". With this hope in mind, he set off for Weimar in 1708.

Left: The Lutheran parson and poet, Erdmann Neumeister, composed texts for church cantatas which influenced Bach during his years at Weimar.
The words for these cantatas, as for chorales, were sometimes adapted from the Bible or newly written on religious themes.

Left: The splendid organ built by Gottfried Silbermann (1683–1753) in the Hofkirche, Dresden. The Baroque organ, of which this is a fine example, is able to do justice to accompanied melody and to many tunes at once, for it has a blended collection of stops and a completely independent pedal.

Below: A church cantata being performed in Germany in the early 18th century. Some of the instruments shown are those which Bach would have heard at Buxtehude's concerts in Lübeck. Notice the conductor with two batons keeping the music together since the singers were often some distance away.

The Baroque Tradition

In its most general sense, the term Baroque covers the period between 1620 and 1750. The Thirty Years War (1618–1648) had devastated much of Germany, while the Civil War in England (1642–1651) had turned the old order upside-down. Such great changes were difficult to face. So it is not surprising that the rulers of Europe tried to escape to an ideal world, through the creations of the painters, sculptors, architects and musicians in their service.

Within this world, no expense was spared to glorify the patrons: monarchy, aristocracy and Church. More than in any other age, artists of all kinds worked together – painter with set-designer, writer with musician – to produce court entertainment on a spectacular scale. No wonder the stage was so important; for here the arts could combine. Music became of equal importance to words, and operas were born from the old stylized masques and ballets.

It is impossible to exaggerate the splendor of the courts, within which, like a kind of play within a play, the king, queen, elector, or prince, and the nobility were invited onto the stages of their own theaters to act out mythical or historical roles. In Restoration England, lighthearted and fanciful comedies were popular too. The characters were an exaggerated mirror of their audience, always ready with witty and clever remarks. The sharp tongue of the theater suited the age, for it poked fun at dullness of all kinds.

Baroque architecture, which grew out of Rome in the 1620s, combined classical features with ornate decoration. The church of St. Peter's in Rome and the palaces of Blenheim and Versailles are splendid examples. As the period wore on, Baroque art became more elaborate and fantastically decorated, growing into a style called Rococo. Examples include Pope's poem *The Rape of the Lock* and Watteau's painting *Embarkation for Cythera*.

Left: Henry Purcell (1659–1695) was, at 23, organist at the Chapel Royal in St. James's, London. Later, he moved to Westminster Abbey where, as well as playing the organ, he wrote a great deal of church music. He also composed works that were not religious, like Dido and Aeneas.

Below left: George Frederick Handel (1685–1759) was born in Halle, Germany, but spent most of his life in England. Unlike Bach, Handel was extremely popular in his own time and always managed to adapt his music to suit public taste. His works include the Messiah, *and the* Water Music.

Right: Bernini's statue of St. Teresa (1644) in the Church of St-Maria della Vittoria in Rome. Bernini has been called the creator of the Baroque style. The energy and movement of the figures and their three-dimensional quality make this a religious masterpiece.

Left: A painting by Canaletto (1697–1768) of St. Mark's Square in Venice. Monteverdi worked in the Basilica of St. Mark's (left). Opera flourished in the city, which itself looks like an elaborate stage set.

Below: Antonio Vivaldi (c1678–1741) was a Venetian composer and violinist. He wrote over 40 operas, but it was his work as an instrumental composer which influenced Bach. Georg Philip Telemann (1681–1767) was a German composer, working mainly in Leipzig and Hamburg. He was offered Bach's post as Cantor at St. Thomas's, but turned it down.

Monteverdi

Lully

Vivaldi

Telemann

Above: Claudio Monteverdi (1567–1643) was an important Italian composer, not only of some of the earliest and finest operas (Orfeo, 1607), but of much dramatic church music. His music is in the Italian style: highly decorated and often intensely moving. Jean Baptiste Lully (1632–1687) was the director of string players and dancing master at Louis XIV's Court.

Right: The Palace of Versailles; designed by Mansart for Louis XIV. The elaborate, formal gardens and avenues match the rich, highly decorated interior of the palace.

Musician to the Princes

Bach was first introduced to court music when he visited the Court of Celle, near Lüneburg, while he was still at school. There the French wife of Duke Georg Wilhelm, Eleanore, had created a miniature Versailles. She employed French musicians who played in their own elaborate, ornamental style, far removed from the German church tradition in which Bach had grown up.

Bach's first court post was as violinist in the orchestra of Duke Johann Ernst of Weimar. After working in Arnstadt and Mühlhausen, he returned to the court of his first employer's younger brother, Wilhelm Ernst, in 1708, with an income already double what he had earned at Mühlhausen. To begin with, it was his duty to look after the Duke's musical establishment and a select band of string players. But in 1714 Bach was appointed Konzertmeister, second only to the Kapellmeister, or chief musician. He now had to compose a new cantata each month, in addition to rehearsing the musicians and giving lessons to the Duke's nephews, Ernst August and Johann Ernst. It was they who introduced him to the Italian music of the time, a style depending for effect on contrasts between different groups, large and small, loud and soft, rather than on the ornamentation of a melody. Bach amused his pupils by altering concertos by Vivaldi to suit the instruments at hand. To begin with, at least, it was a productive time for Bach. But in 1716, the Kapellmeister, Drese, died and instead of Bach, the Duke chose Drese's son, a third-rate musician, to succeed him. Bach was bitterly disappointed, and eagerly accepted when the younger of the nephews, Ernst August, arranged for him to be offered the post of Kapellmeister at his brother-in-law's court at Köthen. This made the Duke so angry that at first he would not allow Bach to go, and placed him under arrest for almost a month. Then, grudgingly, he was set free to make his way northeast to Köthen.

The Challenge with Marchand

In the autumn of 1717, Bach went to Dresden and found that his visit coincided with that of the famous harpsichordist, Louis Marchand. Dismissed from the French Court in disgrace earlier that year, Marchand, sure of his superiority, eagerly agreed to a competition with Bach. Hearing him play, however, Marchand lost his nerve. On the morning of the contest, while Bach, the judges and a large audience waited impatiently, it was discovered that Marchand had sped out of Dresden that morning by fast coach, too arrogant to stay and face certain defeat. So Bach played alone, and delighted and amazed his audience.

Right: Duke Wilhelm Ernst of Weimar, Bach's patron for whom he worked from 1708 to 1717. At the age of seven, he preached a sermon to his courtiers and he remained deeply and sternly religious. He lived simply at his court, where all the lights were put out at 8 p.m. in winter and 9 p.m. in summer.

Right: Bach's other patron, Prince Leopold of Anhalt-Köthen, could not have been more different. He loved music for its own sake practiced constantly. The lights of his palace must often have burned late into the night, while concerts and dances were performed.

Life at Köthen was very different. Prince Leopold, a keen and gifted player of the viola da gamba, violin and harpsichord, worked closely with Bach as a friend and fellow musician rather than as an employer. Without the petty irritations of his time as organist, Bach was at last able to write freely for first-class musicians who were quick to appreciate and to master his compositions. This is the period of his great orchestral and chamber music and much keyboard music too. But tragedy struck. On returning from Karlsbad with the Prince after a two-month stay, Bach found his wife, whom he had left in good health, dead and already buried. His four children, all under 12, were left alone. Like his father before him, Bach sought to marry again for his children's sake. In December 1721, Anna Magdalena, a young singer at the castle, became his wife. He was to write much music for her and their children, including the famous *Anna Magdalena's Notebook*.

Unhappily, his new found peace was not destined to last. A week after his own marriage, the Prince married a cousin, Frederica Henrietta, who showed no interest at all in music, and positively resented her husband practicing so much of the time. Within a year, she had made life so difficult for Bach, that he left to take up a position as Cantor at St. Thomas's Church in Leipzig.

Above: A view of Prince Leopold's castle at Köthen. Bach received almost the highest salary there because of the high esteem in which music was held.

Right: Christian Ludwig, Margrave of Brandenburg.

Below: The beginning of the first of six concertos which Bach dedicated to the Margrave of Brandenburg in 1721.

Life in Leipzig

Despite Bach's growing reputation both as an organist and as an expert adviser on the building and renovation of organs, his reception in Leipzig was not an especially warm one. The authorities had wanted to employ Telemann as Cantor of St. Thomas's, but he turned down the offer. It was this which led to the council's famous comment: "Since we cannot get the best man, we must make do with the second best." It is not to their credit that they never realized how wrong they were. Having heard the first performance of Bach's *St. John Passion* on Good Friday, a fortnight before his appointment, they put a clause in the contract to the effect that his music should neither be "too lengthy nor operatic in style". This was one of 14 points to which Bach had promised to adhere when he signed it in May 1723. He was less free in other ways too. After his luxurious quarters at Köthen, it must have taken time to get used to the cramped conditions at the school, where his composing room was separated from a junior classroom by a thin partition.

The city of Leipzig, however, must have delighted Bach. A rich and cultured town with a famous university, it was also a busy commerical center; renowned for its printing and publishing.

Above: A romantic view of the Bach family in Leipzig. "All my children are born musicians," wrote Bach to his schoolfriend Erdmann in 1730, "from my own family, I assure you I can arrange a good vocal and instrumental concert."

Below: A view of the Rathaus (the Town Hall) in Leipzig, as it was in Bach's day. The marketplace (foreground) was the center of activity in the town.

There were beautiful buildings and some of the houses of the rich were timber-framed and ingeniously carved and decorated. Opera, recently introduced to the city, was flourishing, and there was an excellent company performing comic plays. The affairs of the town were managed by a high court which met quarterly, and a council judged church matters. It was to this council that Bach was answerable.

The university, as well as drawing many intelligent men to the city, was active in many societies to which townspeople could belong. There were two principal musical societies; and Bach became the conductor of one of them. It met each week, in a garden in summer and in a coffee house in winter.

The presence of the university was a great help to Bach. Musicians who were studying, were both happy to perform in the church orchestra when necessary, and to play other music which Bach was writing. This was, more than anything, the period of his great religious compositions.

Right: A clavichord of the 1720s, an instrument which was extremely popular in Bach's day and which responds especially well to his music. Behind the clavichord is the title page from the score of the Well-Tempered Clavier *which Bach wrote around the new system of tuning keyboard instruments.*

Bach the Teacher

"Anyone could have done as much as I have done if he had worked as hard," wrote Bach who, as well as teaching and composing, had to copy out the parts for each instrument in a piece of music separately. During these busy years the amount of work he did was astonishing, although he found it very hard to readjust to a life of serving church authorities after being the Kapellmeister at Köthen. Once again, he was obliged to rehearse the choir and he encountered the same difficulties and frustrations as at Arnstadt and Mühlhausen. His narrowminded and unhelpful supervisors repeatedly disregarded Bach's requests. They admitted useless singers to the choir and even, at one stage, forbade him to choose his own hymns. Such treatment greatly disheartened the composer, and he must have resented the precious composing time he wasted on these quarrels.

Nevertheless, in 1729, he conducted the first performance of his *St. Matthew Passion*, cleverly setting the choral and orchestral parts to relatively easy music which could be performed by his own church players backed up by amateurs – towns-

Above: St. Thomas's School in Leipzig where Bach lived and worked from 1723 until his death in 1750. Here Anna Magdalena copied his music so that eventually her script became almost identical to Bach's.

Right: The outstanding trumpeter, Gottfried Reiche, master of the clarino trumpet which is very different from today's valved trumpet. There were no mechanical means for shortening or lengthening the valves as on a modern instrument. Different notes needed different rates of blowing and positions of the mouth. Reiche died suddenly of a stroke the day after a celebration in the presence of the King of Poland, Frederick Augustus III. It is said that he died as a result of this performance, made worse by the smoke of 600 torches.

Left: An engraving (1698) of a cantor teaching his choir, exactly as Bach would have done. Instead of each pupil being given a printed copy of the parts, as would happen today, they would gather round, following the teacher's pointer.

Above: The air on which the Goldberg Variations were composed was first written in Anna Magdalena's Notebook in 1725, as a sarabande in G.

Below: Part of the score of the St. Matthew Passion, first performed in 1729.

people, students and members of the musical society. Punctuating the drama are chorales for the entire congregation to sing.

As well as producing a steady flow of compositions, Bach taught keyboard playing and composing. There had been a tradition of playing with the fingers flat, using only the three middle ones, but Bach taught his pupils to hold all five curved over the keys, relaxed and therefore able to play fast passages. To begin with, his pupils were only allowed to play exercises, but with time they progressed to pieces of Bach's own music. Later they were allowed to tackle the *Inventions*, the *Suites* and finally the *48 Preludes and Fugues*.

In composition, too, Bach was careful and disciplined. He encouraged his pupils to compose in their heads, and not to play about the keyboard until they accidentally struck on something that sounded right. Indeed, those who had no musical ideas of their own were discouraged from composition altogether.

Beyond these commitments, Bach still found time to test new organs. A friend of Bach's, lost in admiration after hearing him play, wrote: "Bach is 30 or 40 players rolled into one . . . Rhythm is in every limb of him, all the harmonies are gathered up in his sensitive ears."

The Last Years

Bach seriously considered leaving Leipzig around 1730, but he was persuaded to stay by the new Rector, Johann Gesner. He was Bach's great ally, protecting him from the critical churchmen, whom Bach described as "strange folk with very little care for music in them".

Gesner's successor could hardly have been more different. Johann Ernesti was full of so-called enlightened ideas, and considered music in church and school a waste of time. Nevertheless, Bach completed his *B minor Mass*, the early movements of which he had dedicated to Augustus III, Elector of Saxony. The six Christmas Sundays of 1734 and 1735 were each given a part of the *Christmas Oratorio*, and by 1742 Bach had published all four parts of his *Klavier-Übung*. The last part contains the matchless *Goldberg Variations* for a harpsichord with two keyboards. It was commissioned by Karl Freiherr von Keyserling, the Russian Ambassador to the Court of Dresden, when Bach visited the city to receive confirmation of his appointment as court composer. This honorary title acted as some protection against the difficulties Bach was facing in Leipzig.

Keyserling was an insomniac and had asked Bach to write music to be played by his harpsichordist, Goldberg, to soothe his sleepless nights. Although Bach had not written harpsichord variations before, he composed 30 of them, combining strict counterpoint with exuberance and lyricism.

Later, Bach set to work on what was to be the last and most extraordinary instrumental work of his life, *The Art of Fugue*. He took the theme given him by King Frederick (see box, right) and set about exploring it exhaustively. However, the work was destined to remain unfinished, for Bach's eyesight was failing. Two unsuccessful eye operations were performed in March and April 1750, which left him weak and nearly blind. At work to the end, revising and composing – dictating when no longer able to write himself – Bach died on the evening of July 28th, 1750 and was buried without a memorial.

Below: An engraving of Dresden (1750). In this enlightened city, Bach was warmly applauded for his recitals on the famous Silbermann organs.

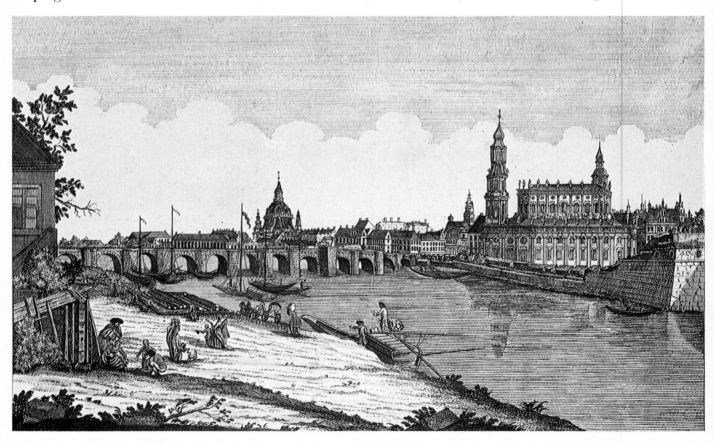

The Musical Offering

Bach's last journey was in 1747 to see his first grandchild, the son of C. P. E. Bach, who was at the time a keyboard player at the Court of Frederick II of Prussia (pictured below). When he arrived at court on May 7th, the King interrupted his music-making to hear Bach play, supplying him with a theme on which to improvise. On his return to Leipzig, Bach enlarged his improvisation into a series of pieces which he sent to the King in Dresden, calling them the *Musical Offering*.

Right: Johann Christian Bach (1735–1782) was the youngest of Anna Magdalena's children. He was taught by C. P. E. Bach, and became music master to Queen Charlotte in England

Right: Carl Philipp Emanuel Bach (1714–1788). He was harpsichordist to King Frederick II of Prussia and the most outstanding teacher of his day. He later became Kapellmeister in Hamburg in 1767 where he influenced Haydn, Mozart and Beethoven.

The Revival

In the 18th century, people only wanted to enjoy what was new in music, believing that it was improving all the time. Musicians were usually commissioned to write for a specific occasion and there was rarely a second performance. Since Bach was considered old-fashioned even when he was alive, it is not surprising that his music was almost forgotten for 50 years after his death.

Mozart had been amazed by a performance of Bach's motet *Sing to the Lord* in 1789, insisting on studying all the separate parts spread out around him. Yet, it was not until the end of the 18th century that any of Bach's music was properly edited and published, most of it for the first time.

Beethoven organized a concert in aid of Bach's only surviving daughter, and Mendelssohn, in 1829, courageously gave the second performance of the *St. Matthew Passion* in Berlin, 100 years after the first. Mendelssohn and Schumann worked tirelessly at making Bach's music known. They organized a Bach Society, so that, by 1900, all of the known works had been published.

Mendelssohn (1809–1847) (left) and Schumann (1810–1856) (above, with his wife, Clara) helped make Bach's music known to the public during the 19th century.

Time Chart

Year	Bach's Life	Other Events
1685	Birth of Handel; In England Charles II dies and James II becomes King.	Birth of Handel and Domenico Scarlatti; In England, Charles II dies and James II becomes King.
1687		The palace of Versailles completed; Lully dies; Newton writes *Principia Mathematica*.
1689		Peter the Great becomes Tsar of Russia; James II abdicates and William and Mary are crowned in England; Henry Purcell writes *Dido and Aeneas*.
1694	Bach's mother, Elizabeth Lämmerhirt, dies.	The Bank of England is started; Queen Mary II of England dies of smallpox; Birth of Voltaire.
1695	Bach's father, Johann Ambrosius, dies; Bach goes to Ohrdruf, to his brother, Johann Christoph.	Death of Purcell and La Fontaine.
1697		Birth of William Hogarth and Antonio Canaletto.
1698	Elias Herda begins to teach Bach.	George Louis becomes Elector of Hanover, later to be King of England (1714).
1699		Death of Racine.
1700	Bach travels to Lüneburg, to be a choirboy at the St. Michael's School	Death of Dryden.
1701		Execution of Captain Kidd, the pirate; The War of Spanish Succession begins; Yale College founded in America.
1702	Bach walks to Hamburg; Visits the Palace of Celle.	William III dies and Anne succeeds to the throne.
1703	Bach works briefly at Weimar, then takes up the position of organist at the New Church, Arnstadt.	Birth of John Wesley, preacher.
1705	Bach granted 4 weeks' leave to hear the great organist and composer, Buxtehude, play at Lübeck. He stays away 4 months.	
1706	In February, Bach returns to Arnstadt.	Benjamin Franklin born; Beginnings of excavations at Pompeii
1707	Bach becomes organist at St. Blasius, Mühlhausen; in October, he marries his cousin, Maria Barbara.	The organist, Buxtehude, dies; Birth of Henry Fielding and Carl Linnaeus.
1708	Bach becomes organist and chamber musician at the court of Duke Wilhelm Ernst of Sachsen-Weimar; His first child, Catherina Dorothea, is born.	
1709	Bach visits Mühlhausen to inaugurate the new organ there.	Birth of Samuel Johnson; First piano built; Beginnings of comic opera in Italy; *Tatler* and *Spectator* founded.
1710	Birth of Bach's son Wilhelm Friedemann.	Handel goes to England; Birth of Robert Boyle, founder of modern chemistry.
1712		Birth of Rousseau; Pope writes *The Rape of the Lock*; Last witchcraft trial takes place in England.
1714	Birth of Bach's son, Carl Philipp Emanuel.	Queen Anne dies and George I, Elector of Hanover, becomes King of England; Fahrenheit invents the mercury thermometer.
1715	Birth of Bach's son, Johann Gottfried Bernhard.	Louis XIV of France, the Sun King, dies.
1716	Drese dies and his son is given the post of Kapellmeister in preference to Bach.	Thomas Gray born.
1717	Bach is arrested by Duke Wilhelm Ernst, and grudgingly released to become Kapellmeister at Köthen; The contest with Marchand takes place in Dresden.	Watteau paints his *Embarkation for Cythera*.
1719	Bach tries in vain to meet Handel in Halle.	Death of Joseph Addison; Defoe writes *Robinson Crusoe*.
1720	Maria Barbara dies.	The South Sea Bubble financial collapse; Building of the Wurzburg Residence begun by Neumann.

Year	Bach's Life	Other Events
1721	Bach composes the *Brandenburg Concertos*; In December he marries his second wife, Anna Magdalena.	St. Martin-in-the-Fields built by Gibbs; Watteau dies.
1722	The first part of the *Well-Tempered Clavier* (24 preludes and fugues) and the first music book for Anna Magdalena are composed.	Death of Reinken; Rameau writes his *Treatise on Harmony*.
1723	The *St. John Passion* is first performed; Bach becomes Cantor at St. Thomas's in Leipzig.	Death of Sir Christopher Wren; Birth of Joshua Reynolds, painter and Adam Smith, economist.
1725	The second music book for Anna Magdalena is composed.	Death of Peter the Great of Russia; Death of Alessandro Scarlatti; Birth of Clive of India.
1726		Swift writes *Gulliver's Travels*; Vivaldi composes *The Four Seasons*.
1727		Death of George I and Isaac Newton; Birth of Gainsborough.
1729	First performance of the *St. Matthew Passion* in St. Thomas's Church on Good Friday.	Death of Congreve, the playwright.
1730	Johann Gesner is appointed Rector of St. Thomas's.	Birth of Edmund Burke, statesman.
1731	Publication of Part I of the *Klavier-Übung*.	Death of Daniel Defoe; Birth of George Washington.
1732	Birth of Bach's son, Johann Christoph Friedrich.	Birth of Haydn; Covent Garden Opera House opens in London.
1733	Bach composes the *B minor Mass*.	
1734	First performance of the *Christmas Oratorio* over the Christmas season.	Frederick Augustus II, Elector of Saxony becomes Frederick Augustus III, King of Poland.
1735	Birth of Bach's son, Johann Christian; Publication of the *Klavier-Übung*, Part II. Composes *Italian Concerto* for harpsichord.	Hogarth draws his *Rake's Progress*; Linnaeus, the naturalist, writes *Systema Naturae*.
1736	Bach appointed court composer to the Elector of Saxony, an honorary post.	Birth of James Watt, inventor of the steam engine.
1739	Publication of the *Klavier-Übung*, Part III.	Handel's oratorios, *Saul* and *Israel in Egypt* are first performed; Dick Turpin, the highwayman, dies.
1740	Carl Philipp Emanuel enters the service of Frederick II, King of Prussia; Bach's eyesight is by now very bad.	Frederick the Great introduces freedom of worship and freedom of the press in Prussia.
1741	Publication of the *Klavier-Übung*, Part IV.	Handel composes the *Messiah*.
1742	Bach composes the *Goldberg Variations*.	Handel's *Messiah* is first performed in Dublin.
1743		Handel writes *Samson*; The architect, Neumann, begins the church of Vierzehnheiligen.
1744	Part II of the *Well-Tempered Clavier* (24 preludes and fugues) is written.	Hogarth draws his *Marriage à la Mode*; Death of Alexander Pope; Birth of Lamarck, the French naturalist.
1745	Birth of Bach's first grandson, Johann August, son of Carl Philipp Emanuel.	Death of Swift; Knobelsdorff begins work on the Sans-souci Palace at Potsdam.
1746		Battle of Culloden; Handel writes *Judas Maccabeus*.
1747	Bach visits Frederick the Great at Potsdam; He improvises on a theme for the King and later dedicates the *Musical Offering* to him.	Birth of Charles James Fox; Richardson writes *Clarissa Harlowe*.
1748	Bach probably begins work on *The Art of Fugue*.	David Hume writes *Philosophical Essays Concerning Human Understanding*.
1749		Birth of Goethe; Henry Fielding writes *Tom Jones*.
1750	Two unsuccessful operations on Bach's eyes leave him almost blind; He dies on July 28th.	Birth of Salieri, Italian composer; First playhouse opens in New York; Population of Europe estimated at 140 million.

Bach's Greatest Works

Church Music:
Christmas Oratorio (1734)
Magnificat in D (c1723)
B minor Mass (1733)
St. John Passion (1723)
St. Matthew Passion (1729)

Orchestral Music:
Six Brandenburg Concertos (1721)
Four Orchestral Suites
Violin Concerto in E major
Violin Concerto in A minor
Double Violin Concerto in D minor

Solo Music:
Six Solo Sonatas (Partitas) for Violin
Six Solo Suites (Sonatas) for Cello

Other Instrumental Music:
Passacaglia in C minor for Organ
Goldberg Variations for Harpsichord (1742)
Italian Concerto for Harpsichord (1735)
Anna Magdalena's Notebook (1722 and 1725)
Six French Suites (c1722)
Six English Suites (c1725)
48 Preludes and Fugues (The Well-Tempered Clavier)
  Book I (1722), Book II (1744)
The Art of Fugue (1748–1750)

Glossary

Cantata A short piece of music for one or more solo singers and an orchestra, and usually sung with a chorus.

Cantor A choirmaster.

Chamber music Music written for small groups of instruments, few enough to play in a room, or chamber.

Choral music Music which is sung.

Chorale A hymn sung in German, introduced by Martin Luther in the Reformation. The words and music were either specially composed or altered from existing verses and tunes.

Concerto A piece ot music in which a solo instrument, such as a violin, plays with an orchestra. A concerto usually has three movements.

Counterpoint The kind of music in which two or more different tunes fit together to form a rich sound.

Fugue A piece of music in which a short melody or theme, called the subject, is repeated by other instruments in a higher or lower key to form counterpoint.

Mass The celebration of the Eucharist in the Roman Catholic Church. The fixed parts of the Mass are the *Kyrie, Gloria, Credo, Sanctus* and *Agnus Dei.* They are called the *Ordinary of the Mass* and are sometimes sung by the congregation. Many composers retained the original Latin and set these parts to music, for example, Bach's *B minor Mass* and Beethoven's *Missa Solemnis.*

Motet A piece of choral music for one or more voices, without instrumental accompaniment.

Opera A play set to music for performance on the stage.

Patron Someone who paid artists and craftsmen of any kind to produce work to his specifications.

Prelude A piece of music played before any other piece which acts as an introduction or preparation for what is to follow.

Rococo An extreme form of the Baroque in which detail became almost more important than the design of the work as a whole.

Sonata A piece of instrumental music, usually with three or four movements.

Index

Note: Page numbers in *italics* refer to illustrations.

Acknowledgements

Picture Research: Elizabeth Rudoff

Photographs: Archiv für Kunst und Geschichte 12 *bottom*, 18 *centre right*, 19 *centre right*, 22 *top*; Bildarchiv d'Osterreichische Nationalbibliothek 9 *bottom*; Bildarchiv Preussischer Kulturbesitz end pages, 4/5, 6, 7, 9 *centre*, 10, 11 *top*, 14 *top and bottom*, 19 *bottom*, 20 *top*, 21 *top*, 23 *top left and right*, 24, 25 *top left*; Deutsche Fotothek, Dresden 18 *left, bottom right*, 23 *bottom*; Giraudon, Paris 17 *bottom*; Mansell Collection 13 *bottom*, 16 *left*, 25 *bottom*; Mary Evans Picture Library 25 *centre right*; Pressfoto Makovec 13 *top*; Museum für beschichte der Stadt Leipzig/R. Funk 22 *bottom*; Scala 16 *bottom right*, 17 *top*, 25 *top right*; ZEFA 12 *top*, 15 *top*.
Cover: Archiv für Kunst und Geschichte.